The Mysteries of Freemasonry and the Druids

By Albert G. Mackey, Manly P. Hall, C. H. Vail
and W. Winwood Reade

Copyright © 2020 Lamp of Trismegistus. All rights reserved. No part of this publication may be reproduced or transmitted in any form or by any means, electronic or mechanical, including photocopying, recording, or by any information storage and retrieval system, without permission in writing from Lamp of Trismegistus. Reviewers may quote brief passages.

ISBN: 978-1-63118-444-4

*Foundations of Freemasonry
Series*

Other Books in this Series and Related Titles

Masonic Symbolism of the Apron & the Altar
by Albert G. Mackey & other authors (978-1-63118-428-4)

Royal Arch, Capitular and Cryptic Masonry
by William F. Kuhn & other authors (978-1-63118-425-3)

Masonic Symbolism of Easter and the Christ in Masonry
by various authors (978-1-63118-434-5)

The Two Great Pillars of Boaz and Jachin
by Albert Mackey, William Harvey & others (978-1-63118-433-8)

Masonic Symbolism of King Solomon's Temple
by Albert G. Mackey & others (978-1-63118-442-0)

Symbolism and Discourses on the Entered Apprentice, Fellowcraft and Master Mason Blue Lodge Degrees by various (978-1-63118-413-0)

The Lost Keys of Freemasonry or The Secret of Hiram Abiff
by Manly P. Hall (978-1-63118-427-7)

Plato and Platonism & Related Esoteric Essays
by H. P. Blavatsky & others (978-1-63118-432-1)

Ancient Egyptian Mysteries and Hieroglyphics, Modern Freemasonry & Initiation of the Pyramid by various (978-1-63118-430-7)

Symbolism of the Corner Stone, the North East Corner and the Religious & Masonic Symbolism of Stones by various (978-1-63118-412-3)

The Philosophy of Masonry in Five Parts by Roscoe Pound
(978-1-63118-004-0)

The Story and Legend of Hiram Abiff by William Harvey, Manly P. Hall and Albert G. Mackey (978-1-63118-411-6)

Audio Versions are also Available on Audible and iTunes

Table of Contents

Introduction…7

Druidism and Freemasonry
by Albert G. Mackey…9

The Druidic Mysteries of Britain and Gaul
by Manly P. Hall…37

The Druidical Mysteries
by C. H. Vail…47

Freemasonry and the Druids
by W. Winwood Reade…51

Introduction

From the beginning of Modern Freemasonry's birthdate of 1717, the intelligentsia of humanity have found refuge for safe reflection within the walls of the fraternity. Masonic writers have produced a nearly incalculable amount of written musings on a multitude of esoteric and philosophical subjects, as they relate to the ancient mysteries that Freemasonry currently storehouses. Sadly, most of it appears to have sat largely unread, as American Freemasonry in particular, continues to transform itself into something that bears little resemblance to what it was originally designed to be. The true essence of Freemasonry is not that of blind patriotism or a single-minded national religion but one of Universal Brotherhood and altruism, designed for the betterment not just of its members but of society as a whole. In particular, for those who are not members of the fraternity, as Freemasonry has always acted as a beacon, to help guide humanity through darker times, with the hopes that one day we will collectively reach a truly enlightened age.

It's not uncommon for new members joining the fraternity to find little education within the walls of many modern lodges, in spite of so much written material available to the membership. Many older members are not simply uneducated with regards to real Masonic history and symbology, not to mention the vast arena of related subjects, but they are disinterested in all of it, as well.

Lamp of Trismegistus is doing its part to help preserve humanity's Masonic history by making some of these classics available to those students who are seeking to unearth the knowledge of these ancient colossi. As such, Lamp of Trismegistus offers its readers highlights of Masonic study, culled from a variety of authors and viewpoints, with the hope bringing education back into the fraternity. So, be sure to check out other titles in our *Foundations of Freemasonry Series* as well as our *Esoteric Classics, Theosophical Classics, Occult Fiction* and our *Christian Apocrypha Series*, and don't be afraid to let a little altruism into your own heart or even into your Lodge. You can also download the audio versions of most of these titles from iTunes or Audible, for learning on the go.

Druidism and Freemasonry

By Albert G. Mackey

Mr. Preston, in commencing his history of Masonry in England, asserts that there are convincing proofs that the science of Masonry was not unknown to the early Britons even before the time of the invasion of the Romans. Hence he suggests the probability that the Druids retained among them many usages similar to those of Masons; but he candidly admits that this is a mere conjecture.

Hutchinson thinks it probable that many of the rites and institutions of the Druids were retained in forming the ceremonies of the Masonic society.

Paine, who knew, by the way, as little of Masonry as he did of the religion of the Druids, dogmatically asserts that "*Masonry is the remains of the religion of the ancient Druids, who, like the Magi of Persia and the priests of Heliopolis in Egypt, were priests of the sun.*"

The learned Faber, a much more competent authority than Paine, expresses the opinion that the Druidical Bards "are probably the real founders of English Freemasonry."

Godfrey Higgins, whose inventive genius, fertile imagination, and excessive credulity render his great work, the

Anacalypsis, altogether unreliable, says that he has "*no doubt that the Masons were Druids, Culidei, or Chaldea, and Casideans.*"

Dr. Oliver, it is true, denies that the Masons of the present day were derived from the Druids. He thinks that the latter were a branch of what he calls the Spurious Freemasonry, which was a secession from the Pure Freemasonry of the Patriarchs. But he finds many analogies in the rites and symbols of the two institutions, which indicate their common origin from a primitive system, namely, the ancient Mysteries of the Pagans.

The theory of those who find a connection either in analogy or by succession between the Druids and the Freemasons accounts for this connection by supposing that the Druids derived their system either from Pythagoras or from the ancient Mysteries through the Phoenicians, who visited Britain at an early period for commercial purposes.

But before we can profitably discuss the relations of Druidism to Freemasonry, or be prepared to determine whether there were any relations whatever between the two, it will be necessary to give a brief sketch of the history and character of the former. This is a topic which, irrespective of any Masonic reference, is not devoid of interest.

Of all the institutions of antiquity, there is none with which we are less acquainted than that of the Druidism of Britain and Gaul. The investigations of recent archaeologists have tended to cast much doubt on the speculations of the antiquaries of the 17th and 18th centuries. Stokely, for instance, one of the most learned of those who have sought to establish out of the stone monuments of England a connected history of Druidism, has been said by Ferguson, in his work on *Rude Stone Monuments*, to have been indebted more to a prolific imagination than to authentic facts for the theory which he has sought to establish.

The skepticism of Ferguson is, however, not less objectionable in a critical inquiry than the credulity of Stokely. There is evidently a middle way between them.

Ferguson can not deny the existence of Druids in Gaul and Britain, since the fact is stated by Caesar. He supposes that there were two distinct races in the island; the original inhabitants, who were of Turanian origin, and, being more uncivilized, were driven by the other race, who were Celts, into the fastnesses of the Welsh hills long before the Roman invasion. Among the former he thinks that the religion of Druidism, consisting of tree and serpent worship, may have been practiced. And he accounts for the error of the classical writers in describing the priests of the latter race as Druids by attributing it to the confounding of the two races by the "uncritical Romans."

Very recently a bold and very skeptical theory has been advanced by Dr. Ignaz Goldziher, in his work on *Mythology Among the Hebrews*, which aims at a total annihilation of Druidism as a system of secret initiation among the ancient Britons (*whose Druidism was only a national religion*), and attributes its invention to the modern Welsh, who created it for the purpose of elevating and strengthening their own nationality in their rivalry with the English. He says:

> *"The Cymri of Wales, becoming alive to the opposition in nationality between themselves and the English, felt the need of finding a justification of this opposition in the oldest prehistoric times. It was then first suggested to them that they were descendants of the ancient, renowned Celtic nation; and to keep alive this Celtic national pride they introduced an institution of New Druids, a sort of secret society like the Freemasons. The New Druids, like the old ones, taught a sort of national religion, which, however, the people having long become Christian and preserved no independent national traditions, they had mostly to invent themselves. Thus arose the so-called Celtic mythology of the god Hu and the goddess Ceridolu (Ceridwen), etc. - mere poetical fictions which never lived in popular belief."*

The questions involved in this difference of opinion are as yet not critically decided, and I shall therefore content myself with giving the views of the history and religion of the Druids as they have been generally received and believed, without confusing the subject with the contending speculations which have been fostered by the credulity or the imagination of one side and impugned by the skepticism of the other.

The Druids, which word signifies magicians, were the priests of the religion of the ancient Britons, among whom they exercised almost unlimited influence and authority. They presided over and directed the education of the youths; they decided without appeal all judicial controversies; they were exempted from all taxes and legal impositions; and whoever refused to submit to their decisions on any question was subjected to excommunication, by which he was forbidden access to the altars or the performance of religious rites, and was debarred from all intercourse with his relatives, his friends, or his countrymen. Hence no superstition was ever more terrible than that of the priest-ridden Britons.

The Druids were under the chief authority of an Archdruid, which office was for life, but originally elective. They were divided into three orders, the highest being the Druids, below which were the *Prophets* and the *Pates or Bards*. They held an annual assembly, at which litigated questions were decided and new laws were made or old ones abrogated. They held also four quarterly meetings, on the days of the equinoxes and the solstices.

They permitted none of their doctrines or ceremonies to be committed to common writing, but used a cipher for their concealment. This, Caesar says, consisted of the letters of the Greek alphabet; a statement by no means probable, since it would infer a knowledge by them of the Greek language, of which we have no evidence.

The opinion of Toland is more plausible - that the characters used were those of the Irish *Ogum* alphabet. Sir James Ware, who wrote in Latin, about the middle of the 17th century, a work on the *Antiquities of Ireland*, says that "*the ancient Irish, besides the vulgar characters, used also various occult or artificial forms of writing, called Ogum, in which they wrote their secrets;*" and he adds that he himself was in possession of an ancient book or parchment filled with these characters.

Their places of worship were, according to the contemporaneous authority of Caesar and Tacitus, in sacred groves. Stokely and other antiquaries of his school suppose that the megalithic monuments found in Britain, such as at Stonehenge and Avebury, were Druidical temples, but Ferguson denies this, and asserts that "*there is no passage in any classical author which connects the Druids either directly or indirectly with any stone temples or stones of any sort.*" The question remains unadjudicated, but the position taken by Ferguson seems to be supported by better archaeological evidence.

Their worship, like that of the ancient Mysteries, was accompanied by a secret initiation. Their doctrines were communicated only to the initiated, who were strictly forbidden to expose them to the profane.

What were the precise forms of this initiation it is impossible to say. The Druids themselves, wedded to their oral system of instruction, have left no records. But Dr. Oliver, depending on inferences that he has drawn from the Welsh triads, from the poem of the ancient bard Taleisin, and some other Cambrian authorities, aided by the inventive genius of his own imagination, has afforded us a very minute, if not altogether accurate, detail of these initiatory ceremonies. The account is entirely too long for reproduction, but a condensed view of it will not be uninteresting.

Previous to admission to the first degree, or that of the *Vates*, the candidate was submitted to a careful preparation, which in especial cases extended to the long period of twenty years.

The ceremony of initiation began by placing the candidate in the *pastos*, chest or coffin, in which he remained enclosed for three days, to represent death, and was liberated or restored to life on the third day.

The sanctuary being now prepared for the business of initiation, the Druids are duly arranged, being appropriately clothed and crowned with ivy. The candidate, representing a blind man, is then introduced while a hymn to the Sun is being chanted. He is placed under the care of an officer whose duty it is to receive him in the land of rest, and he is directed to kindle the fire under the cauldron of Ceridwen, the Druidical goddess. A pageant is then formed, and the candidate makes a circumambulation of nine times around the sanctuary, in circles from east to west by the south. The procession is first slow and amid a death-like silence; at length the pace is increased into a rapid and furious motion, accompanied with the tumultuous clang of musical instruments and the screams of harsh and dissonant voices reciting in verse the praises of those heroes who were brave in war, courteous in peace, and patrons of religion.

This sacred ceremony was followed by the administration of an oath of secrecy, violation of which could be expiated only by death.

Then succeeded a series of ceremonies in which, by means of masks, the candidate was made to assume the character of various animals, such as the dog, the deer, the mare, the cock, etc.

This, according to Oliver, concluded the first part of the ceremony of initiation. The second part began with striking the candidate a violent blow on the head with an oar, and a pitchy darkness immediately ensued, which was soon changed into a blaze of light which illuminated the whole area of the shrine.

This sudden transition from darkness to light was intended to shadow forth the same transition which Noah experienced on emerging from the gloom of the ark to the brightness of the renovated world.

Thus it is contended that the Druids were Arkite worshippers - a concession by Oliver to the theories of Faber and Bryant.

The light was then withdrawn and the candidate was again involved in chaotic darkness. The most dismal howlings, shrieks, and lamentations salute his astonished ear. Thus the figurative death of Noah, typified by his confinement in the ark, was commemorated with every external mark of sorrow. Alarmed at the discordant noises, the candidate naturally sought to escape, but this was rendered impossible, for wherever he turned he was opposed by dogs who pursued him. At length the gigantic goddess Ceridwen seized him and bore him by main force to the mythological sea, which represented the flood of waters over which Noah floated.

Here he is supposed to have remained for a year in the character of Arawn, or Noah. The same appalling sounds continued, until at length, having emerged from the stream, the darkness was removed and the candidate found himself surrounded by the most brilliant coruscations of light. This change produced in the attendants corresponding emotions, which were expressed by shouts and loud paeans that testified their rejoicings at the resuscitation of their god.

The aspirant was then presented to the Archdruid, who explained to him the design of the mysteries and imparted some portion of the secret knowledge of Druidism, and recommended to him the practice of fortitude, which was considered as one of the leading traits of perfection.

With the performance of these painful ceremonies, the first degree of initiation into the Druidical Mysteries was concluded.

In the second degree, where the trials appear, from Oliver's description, to have been of a less severe character, the candidate underwent lustration, or a typical ablution, which was followed by his enlightenment. He was now instructed in the morality of the order; taught that souls are immortal and must live in a future state; solemnly enjoined to the performance of divine worship and the practice of virtue; and was invested with some of the badges of Druidism. Among these was the crystal, the unequivocal test of his initiation. This crystal, or talisman against danger, was manufactured exclusively by the Druids, and its color varied in the three degrees. In the first it was green, in the second blue, and in the third white. The one presented to the aspirant was a combination of these colors.

Beyond the second degree very few advanced. The third was conferred only on persons of rank and consequence, and in it the aspirant passed through still more arduous ceremonies of purification.

The candidate was committed to secluded solitude for a period of nine months, which time was devoted to reflection and to the study of the sciences, so that he might be prepared more fully to understand the sacred truths in which he was about to be instructed. He was again submitted to a symbolic death and regeneration, by ceremonies different from those of the first degree. He was then supposed to represent a newborn infant, and, being placed in a coracle or boat, was committed to the mercy of the waters. The candidate, says Oliver, was actually set adrift in the open sea, and was obliged to depend on his own address and presence of mind to reach the opposite shore in safety.

This was done at night, and this nocturnal expedition, which sometimes cost the candidate his life, was the closing act of his initiation. Should he refuse to undertake it, he was contemptuously rejected and pronounced unworthy of a participation in the honors to which he aspired and for which he was forever afterward ineligible. But if he courageously entered on the voyage and landed safely, he was triumphantly received by the Archdruid and his companions. He was recognized as a Druid, and became eligible for any ecclesiastical, civil or military dignity. "*The whole circle of human science was open to his investigation; the knowledge of divine things was communicated without reserve; he was now enabled to perform the mysterious rites of worship, and had his understanding enriched with an elaborate system of morality.*"

But little is known of the religion of the Druids, on which these ceremonies are supposed to be founded, and concerning that little the opinions of the learned greatly differ. "*Among those institutions*," says Toland, "*which are thought to be irrecoverably lost, one is that of the Druids; of which the learned have hitherto known nothing but by some fragments concerning them out of the Greek and Roman authors.*" Hence the views relating to their true worship have been almost as various as the writers who have discussed them.

Caesar, who derived his knowledge of the Druids, imperfect as it was, from the contemporary priests of Gaul, says that they worshipped as their chief god Mercury, whom they considered as the inventor of all the arts, and after him Apollo, Mars, Jupiter, and Minerva. But the Romans had a habit of applying to all the gods or idols of foreign nations the names and qualities of the deities of their own mythology. Hence his statement will scarcely amount to more than that the Druids worshipped a variety of gods.

Yet Davies, who, notwithstanding his national prejudices and prepossessions, is, from his learning, an authority not to be contemned, concurs in the view of Caesar so far as to say that "*it is an historical fact, that the mythology and the rites of the Druids were the same, in substance, with those of the Greeks and Romans and of other nations which came under their observation.*"

Dionysius the Geographer, another writer of the Augustan age, says that the rites of Bacchus were celebrated in Britain, and Strabo, on the authority of Artemidorus, who wrote a century before Christ, asserts that in an island close to Britain (*probably the isle of Mona, where the Druids held their principal seat*) Ceres and Proserpine were venerated with rites similar to those of Samothracia.

Bryant, who traced all the ancient religions, principally on the basis of etymology, to traditions of the deluge and the worship of the patriarch Noah, conceived, of course, that Druidism was but a part of this universal cult.

Faber, who followed in the footsteps of his learned predecessor, adopted the same hypothesis, and held the doctrine that the Druids were addicted to what he denominated Arkite worship, or the worship of Noah, and that all their religious rites referred to the deluge, death and immortality being typified by the confinement of the patriarch in the ark and his subsequent emergence from it into a new and renovated world, the symbol of the future life.

It will be evident from the description already given of the Druidical initiations as portrayed by Dr. Oliver, that he concurred to a great extent in the views of Bryant and Faber.

Stukely, one of the most learned of English antiquarians, believed that the Druids were addicted to tree and serpent worship, and he adduces as evidence of the truth of this theory the megalithic monuments of Stonehenge and Avebury, in the arrangement of whose stones he thought that he had traced a serpentine form.

On the contrary, Mr. Ferguson scoffs, in language not always temperate, at the views of Stokely, and not only denies the serpentine form of the stone remains in England, as described by that antiquary, but repudiates the hypothesis that the Druids ever erected or had any connection with stone temples or monuments in any part of the world. But as Ferguson adduces nothing but negative arguments in proof of his assertion, and as he even casts some doubt upon the existence of Druids at all in Britain, his views are by no means satisfactory. He has sought to demolish a palace, but he has not attempted to build even a hovel in its place. Repudiating all other theories, he has offered none of his own.

If the Druids did not erect the stone monuments of Britain, who did? Until the contrary is conclusively proved, we have but little hesitation in attributing them to the Druids. But we need not enter into this discussion, which pertains more properly to the province of archaeology than of Freemasonry.

Some writers have held that the Druids were Sun-worshippers, and that the adoration of the solar orb constituted the national religion of the ancient Britons. Hence these theorists are inclined to believe that Stonehenge and Avebury were really observatories, where the worshippers of the Sun might behold his rising, his diurnal course, and his setting.

Mr. Davies, in his *Celtic Researches* and in his *Mythology and Rites of the British Druids*, maintains that there was among them a mutilated tradition of the Noachic deluge, as there was among all heathen nations. The legend was similar to that of the flood of Deucalion, and was derived from Samothrace and the East, having been brought by a colony from one nation to another and preserved without interruption.

Hu, the supreme god of the Druids, he therefore supposes to have been identical with Noah, and he bestows upon him the various attributes that were distributed among the different gods of the more prolific mythology of the Greeks and Romans, all of which, with Bryant and Faber, he considers were allusive to Sun-worship and to the catastrophe of the deluge.

He therefore asserts that the Helio-Arkite god of the Britons, the great *Hu*, was a Pantheon (*a collection of deities*), who under his several titles and attributes comprehended the group of superior gods whom the Greeks and other refined nations separated and arranged in distinct personages.

In propounding his theory that the Druids were of Eastern origin, and that they had brought from that source their religion and their rites, Mr. Davies has been sustained by the opinions of more recent scholars, though they have traced the birthplace to a more distant region than the island of Samothracia.

It is now very generally believed that the Druids were Buddhists, and that they came into Britain with the great tide of emigration from Asia which brought the Aryan race westward into Europe.

If this be true, the religion of India must have greatly degenerated in the course of its migration. It is admitted that the Druids cultivated the art of magic and in their rites were accustomed to sacrifice human victims, both of which practices were repugnant to the philosophic spirit of Buddhism.

The fact is that, notwithstanding the authority of the Welsh Bards and the scanty passages in Caesar, Tacitus, and a few other Roman writers, we are entirely at sea in reference to everything connected with the religious system of Druidism. Almost all on this mysterious subject is guesswork and conjecture - extravagant theories, the only foundation of which is in the imaginations of their framers and bold assertions for the truth of which no competent authority can be given.

Much of the confusion of ideas in respect to the customs and manners of the ancient Britons has arisen from the ignorance of the old writers in supposing that the inhabitants of Britain, at the time of the Roman invasion and long before, were a homogeneous race. The truth is that the island was inhabited by two very distinct races. Those on the coast, derived from the opposite shores of Gaul, Germany, and Scandinavia, were a people who had made some progress in civilization. The interior of the island was populated by the original natives, who were a very uncivilized and even barbarous race, and it was among these that the Druidical religion prevailed and its mystical and inhuman rites were practiced.

Mr. Ferguson, in his elaborate work on *Tree and Serpent Worship*, sustains this view. He says:

> *"From whatever point of view the subject is looked at, it seems almost impossible to avoid the conclusion that there were two races in England - an older and less civilized people, who in the time of the Romans had already been driven by the Celts into the fastnesses of the Welsh hills, and who may have been serpent-worshippers and sacrificers of human victims, and that the ecumenical Romans confounded the two."*

He is, however, in error in supposing that the Romans were ignorant of this fact, for Caesar distinctly alludes to it. He says in his *Gallic War* that "*the interior part of Britain was inhabited by those who were natives of the island*," thus clearly distinguishing the inhabitants of the interior from those who dwelt on the coast and who, he states, "*had passed over from Belgium.*"

In another place he speaks of them as a rude and barbarous race, who in one of their embassies to him describe themselves as a savage and unpolished people wholly unacquainted with Roman customs.

In speaking of the ancient Gauls, M. Thierry, in his history of that people, makes the following remarks, every one of which may be equally attributed to the ancient Britons. He says:

> "*When we attentively examine the character of the facts concerning the religious belief of the Gauls, we are enabled to recognize two systems of ideas, two bodies of symbols and superstitions altogether distinct - in a word, two religions. One of these is altogether sensible, derived from the adoration of the phenomena of nature; and by its forms and by its literal development it reminds us of the polytheism of the Greeks. The other is founded upon a material pantheism, mysterious, metaphysical, and sacerdotal, and presents the most astonishing conformity with the religions of the East. This last has received the name of Druidism, from the Druids who were its founders and priests.*"

To the former religion M. Thierry gives the name of Gaulish polytheism. A similar distinction must have existed in Britain, though our own writers do not seem generally to have carefully observed it. In no other way can we attempt, with any prospect of success, to reconcile the contending traditions in relation to the religion of the ancient Britons. The Roman writers have attributed a polytheistic form of religion to the people of the coast, derived apparently from Greece, the gods having only assumed different names. But this religion was very far removed in its character from the bloody and mysterious rites of the Druids, who seem to have brought the forms and objects, but not the spirit of their sanguinary and mysterious worship from the far East.

The Masonic writers who have sought to trace some connection between Druidism and Freemasonry have unfortunately too much yielded their judgment to their imagination. Having adopted a theory, they have, in their investigations, substituted speculation for demonstration and assumptions for facts. By a sort of Procrustean process of reasoning, they have fitted all sorts of legends and traditions to the length required for their preconceived system.

Preston had said that "*the Druids retained among them many usages similar to those of the Masons,*" and hence he conjectured that there might be an affinity between the rites of the two institutions, leaving his readers, however, to determine the question for themselves.

Godfrey Higgins - of all writers not claiming to write fiction, the most imaginative and the most conjectural - goes a step further and asserts that he has "*no doubt that the Masons were Druids,*" and that they may be "*traced downward to Scotland and York.*" Of this he thinks "*the presumption is very strong.*"

Hutchinson thinks it probable that some of the rites and institutions of the Druids might be retained in forming the ceremonies of the Masonic society.

The theory of Dr. Oliver connected Druidism and Freemasonry in the following way. The reader must be aware, from what has already been said, that the Doctor held that there were two currents of Masonry that came contemporaneously down the stream of time. These were the Pure Freemasonry of the Patriarchs, that passed through the Jewish people to King Solomon and thence onward to the present day, and a schism from this pure system, fabricated by the Pagan nations and developed in the ancient Mysteries, which impure system he called the Spurious Freemasonry of antiquity. From this latter system he supposes Druidism to have been derived.

Therefore, in support of this opinion, he collates in several of his works, but especially in his *History of Initiation*, the rites and ceremonies of the Druids with those of the Eleusinian, Dionysian, and other mysteries of the Pagan nations, and attempts to show that the design of the initiation was identical in all of them and the forms very similar.

But, true to his theory that the Spurious Freemasonry was an impure secession or offshoot from the Pure or Patriarchal system, he denies that modern Freemasonry has derived anything from Druidism, but admits that similarity in the design and form of initiation in both which would naturally arise from the origin of both from a common system in remote antiquity.

We have therefore to consider two theories in reference to the connection of Druidism and Masonry.

The first is that Freemasonry has derived its system from that of the British Druids. The second is that, while any such descent or succession of the one system from the other is disclaimed, yet that there is a very great similarity in the character of both which points to some common origin.

I shall venture, before concluding this essay, to advance a third theory, which I think is far more reconcilable than either of the others with the true facts of history.

The second of these theories may be dismissed with the remark that it depends for its support on the truth of the theory that there was any kind of historical connection between the Mysteries of the Pagans and Freemasonry. But I think it has been conclusively proved that any similarity of form or design in these institutions is to be attributed not to any dependence or succession, but simply to the influences of that law of human thought which makes men always pursue the same ends by the same methods.

Dr. Oliver has gone so far in the attempt to sustain his theory of two systems of Masonry existing at the same time as to assert that at the time of the Roman invasion, and after the establishment of Christianity in the island, the True and the

Spurious Freemasonry - that is, the Masonic system as now practiced and the impure Masonry of Druidism - "*flourished at the same period and were considered as distinct institutions in Britain.*"

Of the truth of this statement, there is not a scintilla of historical testimony. Even if we were to accept the doctrine of Anderson, that all great architects in past times were Freemasons, we could hardly dignify the rude carpenters of the early Britons and Anglo-Saxons with the title of Masonry.

The first of the theories to which I have alluded, which derives Freemasonry, or at least its rites and ceremonies, from Druidism, will require a more extended review.

In the first place, we must investigate the methods by which it is supposed that the Greeks and Pythagoras communicated a knowledge of their mysteries to the Druids in their secluded homes in uncivilized Britain.

It is supposed that the principal seats of the British Druids were in Cornwall, in the islands adjacent to its coast, in Wales, and in the island of Mona; that is to say, on the southwestern shores of the island.

It is evident that in these localities they were accessible to any of the navigators from Europe or Asia who should have penetrated to that remote distance for the purpose of commerce. Now, just such a class of navigators was found in the Phoenicians, an adventurous people who were distinguished for their spirit of maritime enterprise.

The testimony of the Greek and Roman writers is, that in their distant voyages in search of traffic the Phoenicians had penetrated to the southwestern shores of Britain, and that they loaded their vessels with tin, which was found in great abundance in Cornwall and the Scilly islands on its coast.

The theorists who suppose that the religious rites practiced by the Phoenicians at home were introduced by them into Britain are required, in proof of their theory, to show that the Phoenicians were missionaries as well as merchants; that they remained long enough in Britain, at each voyage, to implant their own religious rites in the island; that these merchant-sailors, whose paramount object was evidently the collection of a valuable and profitable cargo, would divert any portion of the time appropriated to this object to the propagation among the barbarians, whom they encountered in the way of business, of the dogmas of their own mystical religion; that if they were so disposed, the Britons were inclined during these necessarily brief visitations to exchange their ancient religion, whatever it was, for the worship attempted to be introduced by the newcomers; and, finally, that the fierce and sanguinary superstition of the Druids, with its human sacrifices, bore any resemblance to or could have possibly been derived from the purer and more benign religion of the Phoenicians.

For not one of these points is there a single testimony of history, and over every one of them there is cast an air of the greatest improbability. History tells us only that the Phoenician merchants visited Britain for the purpose of obtaining tin. On this the Masonic theorists have erected a fanciful edifice of missionary enterprises successfully ending in the implanting of a new religion.

Experience shows us how little in this way was ever accomplished or even attempted by the modern navigators who visited the islands of the Pacific and other unknown countries for the purposes of discovery. Nor can we be ignorant of how little progress in the change of the religion of any people has ever been effected by the efforts of professed missionaries who have lived and labored for, years among the people whom they sought to convert. They have made, it is true, especial converts, but in only a very few exceptional instances have they succeeded in eradicating the old faith of a nation or a tribe and in establishing their own in its place. It is not to be presumed that the ancient Phoenician merchants could, with less means and less desires, have been more successful than our modern missionaries.

For these reasons, I hold that the proposition that Druidism was introduced from Greece and Asia into Britain by the Phoenicians is one that is wholly untenable on any principle of historic evidence or of probable conjecture.

It has also been asserted that Pythagoras visited Britain and instructed the inhabitants especially in the doctrine of metempsychosis, or the transmigration of souls.

There is, however, not the slightest historical evidence that the sage of Samos ever penetrated in his travels as far as Britain. Nor is it certain that the dogma of the transmigration as taught by him is of the same character as that which was believed by the Druids. Besides, it is contrary to all that we know of the course pursued by Pythagoras in his visits to foreign countries. He went to learn the customs of the people and to acquire a knowledge of whatever science they might possess. Had he visited Britain, which, however, he never did, it would have been to receive and not to impart instruction.

As to the further explanation offered by these theorists, of a connection between Druidism and Masonry, that the former acquired a knowledge of the Eleusinian and other rites in consequence of their communication with the Greeks, during the celebrated invasion of the Celts, which extended to Delphos, and during the intercourse of the Gauls with the Grecian colony of Marseilles, it is sufficient to say that neither of these events occurred until after the system of Druidism must have been well established among the people of Britain and of Gaul.

But the great argument against any connection of Druidism and Freemasonry is not only the dissimilarity of the two systems, but their total repugnance to each other. The sanguinary superstition of the Druids was developed in their sacrifice of human victims as a mode of appeasing their offended deities, and their doctrine of a future life was entirely irreconcilable with the pure belief in immortality which is taught in Freemasonry and developed in its symbols.

The third theory to which I have referred, and which I advanced in the place of the two others which I have rejected, traces Druidism neither to the Phoenicians, nor to Pythagoras, nor to the Greeks. It is that the ancient inhabitants of Britain were a part of the Celtic division of that great Cimmerian race who, springing from their Aryan origin in the Caucasian mountains, first settled for a time in the region of Asia, which lies around the Euxine Sea, and then passed over into the north and west of Europe. One detachment of them entered Gaul, and another, crossing the German Ocean, made their home in Britain.

It is not at all improbable that these nomadic tribes carried with them some memories of the religious faith, which they had learned from the original stock whence they sprung. But there is no fact more patent in ethnology than that of the tendency of all nomadic races springing from an agricultural one to degenerate in civilization.

It has been said that the Druids were Buddhists. This might be so, for Brahmanism and its schism, Buddhism, were the religions of the early Aryan stock whence the Druids descended. But it is very evident that in the course of their migrations the faith of their fathers must have become greatly corrupted. Between Buddhism and Druidism the only connecting link is the dogma of the transmigration of souls. Between the rites of the two sects there is no similarity.

I suppose, therefore, that the system of Druidism was the pure invention of the Britons, just as the Mysteries of Osiris were the fabrication of some Egyptian priest or body of priests. What assistance the Britons had in the formation of their mystical system must have been derived from dim recollections of the dogmas of their fatherland, which, however, from the very dimness of those recollections, must have been greatly perverted. I do not find any authentic proof or any reasonable probability that they had obtained any suggestions in the fabrication or the improvement of their system of religious rites from the Phoenicians, from the Greeks, or from Pythagoras.

If, for the sake of argument, we accept for a time the theory that Freemasonry and the Mysteries originated from a common source, whence is derived a connection between the two, we can not fail to see, on an examination of the doctrines and ceremonies of the Druids, that they bore no relation to those of the Mysteries of Egypt or of Greece. Hence the link is withdrawn which would connect Druidism with Freemasonry through the initiations of the East.

But the fact is that there is not in Druidism the slightest resemblance to Freemasonry except in the unimportant circumstance that both have mystical ceremonies. The voyages of the candidate in Druidism, after a period of long solitude and confinement, his pursuit by the angry goddess Ceridwen and her accompanying dogs, his dangerous passage in a coracle or small boat over the rough waters, and his final landing and reception by the Archdruid, may have referred, as Dr. Oliver thought, to the transmigration of the soul through different bodies, but just as probably symbolized the sufferings and vicissitudes of human life in the progress to intellectual and moral perfection. But they bear not the slightest analogy to the mystical death in Freemasonry, which is the symbol of a resurrection to a future and immortal life.

Hence the bold assertion of Payne, in his frivolous *Essay on the Origin of Freemasonry*, that "*it is derived from and is the remains of the religion of the ancient Druids*," simply shows that he was a mere sciolist in the subject of what he presumptuously sought to treat. Equally untenable is the proposition of the more learned Faber, when he says that "*the Druids are probably the real founders of English Freemasonry.*"

The conclusion to which I think we must arrive, from what we learn of the two institutions from historical knowledge of one and personal experience of the other, is that Freemasonry has no more relation or reference or similitude to Druidism than the pure system of Christianity has to the barbarous Fetichism of the tribes of Africa.

The Druidic Mysteries of Britain and Gaul

By Manly P. Hall

"The original and primitive inhabitants of Britain, at some remote period, revived and reformed their national institutes. Their priest, or instructor, had hitherto been simply named Gwydd, but it was considered to have become necessary to divide this office between the national, or superior, priest and another whose influence [would] be more limited. From henceforth the former became Der-Wydd (Druid), or superior instructor, and [the latter] Go-Wydd, or O-Vydd (Ovate), subordinate instructor; and both went by the general name of Beirdd (Bards), or teachers of wisdom. As the system matured and augmented, the Bardic Order consisted of three classes, the Druids, Beirdd Braint, or privileged Bards, and Ovates." (See Samuel Meyrick and Charles Smith, The Costume of The Original Inhabitants of The British Islands.)

The origin of the word Druid is under dispute. Max Müller believes that, like the Irish word Drui, it means "the men of the oak trees." He further draws attention to the fact that the forest gods and tree deities of the Greeks were called dryades. Some believe the word to be of Teutonic origin; others ascribe it to the Welsh. A few trace it to the Gaelic druidh, which means "a wise man" or "a sorcerer." In Sanskrit the word dru means "timber."

At the time of the Roman conquest, the Druids were thoroughly ensconced in Britain and Gaul. Their power over the people was unquestioned, and there were instances in which armies, about to attack each other, sheathed their swords when ordered to do so by the white-robed Druids. No undertaking of great importance was scatted without the assistance of these patriarchs, who stood as mediators between the gods and men. The Druidic Order is deservedly credited with having had a deep understanding of Nature and her laws. The Encyclopedia Britannica states that geography, physical science, natural theology, and astrology were their favorite studies. The Druids had a fundamental knowledge of medicine, especially the use of herbs and simples. Crude surgical instruments also have been found in England and Ireland. An odd treatise on early British medicine states that every practitioner was expected to have a garden or back yard for the growing of certain herbs necessary to his profession. Eliphas Levi, the celebrated transcendentalist, makes the following significant statement:

> "The Druids were priests and physicians, curing by magnetism and charging amulets with their fluidic influence. Their universal remedies were mistletoe and serpents' eggs, because these substances attract the astral light in a special manner. The solemnity with which mistletoe was cut down drew upon this plant the popular confidence and rendered it powerfully magnetic. * * * The progress of magnetism will someday reveal to us the absorbing properties of mistletoe. We shall then understand the secret of those spongy growths which

drew the unused virtues of plants and become surcharged with tinctures and savors. Mushrooms, truffles, gall on trees, and the different kinds of mistletoe will be employed with understanding by a medical science, which will be new because it is old * * * but one must not move quicker than science, which recedes that it may advance the further." (See *The History of Magic*.)

Not only was the mistletoe sacred as symbolic of the universal medicine, or panacea, but also because of the fact that it grew upon the oak tree. Through the symbol of the oak, the Druids worshiped the Supreme Deity; therefore, anything growing upon that tree was sacred to Him. At certain seasons, according to the positions of the sun, moon, and stars, the Arch-Druid climbed the oak tree and cut the mistletoe with a golden sickle consecrated for that service. The parasitic growth was caught in white cloths provided for the purpose, lest it touch the earth and be polluted by terrestrial vibrations. Usually a sacrifice of a white bull was made under the tree.

The Druids were initiates of a secret school that existed in their midst. This school, which closely resembled the Bacchic and Eleusinian Mysteries of Greece or the Egyptian rites of Isis and Osiris, is justly designated the Druidic Mysteries. There has been much speculation concerning the secret wisdom that the Druids claimed to possess. Their secret teachings were never written, but were communicated orally to specially prepared candidates. Robert Brown, 32°, is of the opinion that the British priests secured their information from Tyrian and Phœnician navigators who, thousands of years before the Christian Era, established colonies in Britain and Gaul while searching for tin. Thomas Maurice, in his Indian Antiquities, discourses at length on Phœnician, Carthaginian, and Greek expeditions to the British Isles for the purpose of procuring tin. Others are of the opinion that the Mysteries as celebrated by the Druids were of Oriental origin, possibly Buddhistic.

The proximity of the British Isles to the lost Atlantis may account for the sun worship which plays an important part in the rituals of Druidism. According to Artemidorus, Ceres and Persephone were worshiped on an island close to Britain with rites and ceremonies similar to those of Samothrace. There is no doubt that the Druidic Pantheon includes a large number of Greek and Roman deities. This greatly amazed Cæsar during his conquest of Britain and Gaul, and caused him to affirm that these tribes adored Mercury, Apollo, Mars, and Jupiter, in a manner similar to that of the Latin countries. It is almost certain that the Druidic Mysteries were not indigenous to Britain or Gaul, but migrated from one of the more ancient civilizations.

The school of the Druids was divided into three distinct parts, and the secret teachings embodied therein are practically the same as the mysteries concealed under the allegories of Blue Lodge Masonry. The lowest of the three divisions was that of Ovate (Ovydd). This was an honorary degree, requiring no special purification or preparation. The Ovates dressed in green, the Druidic color of learning, and were expected to know something about medicine, astronomy, poetry if possible, and sometimes music. An Ovate was an individual admitted to the Druidic Order because of his general excellence and superior knowledge concerning the problems of life.

The second division was that of Bard (Beirdd). Its members were robed in sky-blue, to represent harmony and truth, and to them was assigned the labor of memorizing, at least in part, the twenty thousand verses of Druidic sacred poetry. They were often pictured with the primitive British or Irish harp--an instrument strung with human hair, and having as many strings as there were ribs on one side of the human body. These Bards were often chosen as teachers of candidates seeking entrance into the Druidic Mysteries. Neophytes wore striped robes of blue, green, and white, these being the three sacred colors of the Druidic Order.

The third division was that of Druid (Derwyddon). Its particular labor was to minister to the religious needs of the people. To reach this dignity, the candidate must first become a Bard Braint. The Druids always dressed in white--symbolic of their purity, and the color used by them to symbolize the sun.

In order to reach the exalted position of Arch-Druid, or spiritual head of the organization, it was necessary for a priest to pass through the six successive degrees of the Druidic Order. (The members of the different degrees were differentiated by the colors of their sashes, for all of them wore robes of white.) Some writers are of the opinion that the title of Arch-Druid was hereditary, descending from father to son, but it is more probable that the honor was conferred by ballot election. Its recipient was chosen for his virtues and integrity from the most learned members of the higher Druidic degrees.

According to James Gardner, there were usually two Arch-Druids in Britain, one residing on the Isle of Anglesea and the other on the Isle of Man. Presumably there were others in Gaul. These dignitaries generally carried golden scepters and were crowned with wreaths of oak leaves, symbolic of their authority. The younger members of the Druidic Order were clean-shaven and modestly dressed, but the more aged had long gray beards and wore magnificent golden ornaments. The educational system of the Druids in Britain was superior to that of their colleagues on the Continent, and consequently many of the Gallic youths were sent to the Druidic colleges in Britain for their philosophical instruction and training.

Eliphas Levi states that the Druids lived in strict abstinence, studied the natural sciences, preserved the deepest secrecy, and admitted new members only after long probationary periods. Many of the priests of the order lived in buildings not unlike the monasteries of the modern world. They were associated in groups like ascetics of the Far East. Although celibacy was not demanded of them, few married. Many of the Druids retired from the world and lived as recluses in caves, in rough-stone houses, or in little shacks built in the depths of a forest. Here they prayed and medicated, emerging only to perform their religious duties.

James Freeman Clarke, in his Ten Great Religions, describes the beliefs of the Druids as follows: "The Druids believed in three worlds and in transmigration from one to the other: In a world above this, in which happiness predominated; a world below, of misery; and this present state. This transmigration was to punish and reward and also to purify the soul. In the present world, said they, Good and Evil are so exactly balanced that man has the utmost freedom and is able to choose or reject either. The Welsh Triads tell us there are three objects of metempsychosis: to collect into the soul the properties of all being, to acquire a knowledge of all things, and to get power to conquer evil. There are also, they say, three kinds of knowledge: knowledge of the nature of each thing, of its cause, and its influence. There are three things which continually grow less: darkness, falsehood, and death. There are three which constantly increase: light, life, and truth."

Like nearly all schools of the Mysteries, the teachings of the Druids were divided into two distinct sections. The simpler, a moral code, was taught to all the people, while the deeper, esoteric doctrine was given only to initiated priests. To be admitted to the order, a candidate was required to be of good family and of high moral character. No important secrets were entrusted to him until he had been tempted in many ways and his strength of character severely tried. The Druids taught the people of Britain and Gaul concerning the immortality of the soul. They believed in transmigration and apparently in reincarnation. They borrowed in one life, promising to pay back in the next. They believed in a purgatorial type of hell where they would be purged of their sins, afterward passing on to the happiness of unity with the gods. The Druids taught that all men would be saved, but that some must return to earth many times to learn the lessons of human life and to overcome the inherent evil of their own natures.

Before a candidate was entrusted with the secret doctrines of the Druids, he was bound with a vow of secrecy. These doctrines were imparted only in the depths of forests and in the darkness of caves. In these places, far from the haunts of men, the neophyte was instructed concerning the creation of the universe, the personalities of the gods, the laws of Nature, the secrets of occult medicine, the mysteries of the celestial bodies, and the rudiments of magic and sorcery. The Druids had a great number of feast days. The new and full moon and the sixth day of the moon were sacred periods. It is believed that initiations took place only at the two solstices and the two equinoxes. At dawn of the 25th day of December, the birth of the Sun God was celebrated.

The secret teachings of the Druids are said by some to be tinctured with Pythagorean philosophy. The Druids had a Madonna, or Virgin Mother, with a Child in her arms, who was sacred to their Mysteries; and their Sun God was resurrected at the time of the year corresponding to that at which modern Christians celebrate Easter.

Both the cross and the serpent were sacred to the Druids, who made the former by cutting off all the branches of an oak tree and fastening one of them to the main trunk in the form of the letter T. This oaken cross became symbolic of their superior Deity. They also worshiped the sun, moon, and stars. The moon received their special veneration. Caesar stated that Mercury was one of the chief deities of the Gauls. The Druids are believed to have worshiped Mercury under the similitude of a stone cube. They also had great veneration for the Nature spirits (fairies, gnomes, and undines), little creatures of the forests and rivers to whom many offerings were made. Describing the temples of the Druids, Charles Heckethorn, in The Secret Societies of All Ages & Countries, says:

"Their temples wherein the sacred fire was preserved were generally situate on eminences and in dense groves of oak, and assumed various forms--circular, because a circle was the emblem of the universe; oval, in allusion to the mundane egg, from which issued, according to the traditions of many nations, the universe, or, according to others, our first parents; serpentine, because a serpent was the symbol of Hu, the Druidic Osiris; cruciform, because a cross is an emblem of regeneration; or winged, to represent the motion of the Divine Spirit. * * * Their chief deities were reducible to two--a male and a female, the great father and mother--Hu and Ceridwen, distinguished by the same characteristics as belong to Osiris and Isis, Bacchus and Ceres, or any other supreme god and goddess representing the two principles of all Being."

Godfrey Higgins states that Hu, the Mighty, regarded as the first settler of Britain, came from a place which the Welsh Triads call the Summer Country, the present site of Constantinople. Albert Pike says that the Lost Word of Masonry is concealed in the name of the Druid god Hu. The meager information extant concerning the secret initiations of the Druids indicates a decided similarity between their Mystery school and the schools of Greece and Egypt. Hu, the Sun God, was murdered and, after a number of strange ordeals and mystic rituals, was restored to life.

There were three degrees of the Druidic Mysteries, but few successfully passed them all. The candidate was buried in a coffin, as symbolic of the death of the Sun God. The supreme test, however, was being sent out to sea in an open boat. While undergoing this ordeal, many lost their lives. Taliesin, an ancient scholar, who passed through the Mysteries, describes the initiation of the open boat in Faber's Pagan Idolatry. The few who passed this third degree were said to have been "born again," and were instructed in the secret and hidden truths which the Druid priests had preserved from antiquity. From these initiates were chosen many of the dignitaries of the British religious and political world. (For further details, see Faber's *Pagan Idolatry*, Albert Pike's *Morals and Dogma*, and Godfrey Higgins' *Celtic Druids*.)

The Druidical Mysteries

By C. H. Vail

The Druidical Mysteries were the same as the Celtic, and were celebrated in many countries. We are told by Caesar that these Mysteries were better understood in Britain than anywhere else.

All temples, in whatever country, had places of Initiation connected with them, and they were usually subterranean. The great grotto at Castleton in Derbyshire bears evidence that the celebration of the Druidical Mysteries was of an elaborate nature; the temple at Abury was also a stupendous structure, and was built in the form of a circle.

The periods of Initiation were quarterly and were held at the time of the equinoxes and solstices. There were three degrees in the Druidical Mysteries- Eubatea, Bards, and Druids, and it was obligatory that the candidate for Initiation be well qualified and duly prepared- mental and moral perfection being the first requisite. When the candidate had passed the probationary stage he was clad in a robe, striped with white, blue, and green, emblematical of light, truth, and hope, and confined in a cromlech (tomb) for parts of three days without food, dead, in the language of the Mysteries, after which he was liberated for Initiation, and restored to life on the third day. This confinement preceded his Initiation into each of the two first degrees. When the Aspirant was liberated he was placed in the hands of an officer and con- ducted around the sanctuary nine times, at first with slow and measured step, which at length was in- creased to a rapid pace. During the circuits there was a clang of musical instruments and recitations in praise of those who were heroic in war, courteous in peace, and the friends of religion. At the completion of this ceremony the oath of secrecy was administered and the aspirant then went through various ceremonies in which he represented many characters, declaring among other things, "I have died," and "I have revived," alluding to his mystical death and resurrection.

In the second part of the ceremony there was the dismal darkness, the direful shrieks, the barking dogs, etc., with which we have been made familiar in the preceding Mysteries. The aspirant finally emerged from the gloom, and found himself surrounded with the most brilliant coruscations of light, being then presented to the Archdruid, who instructed him in the Mysteries, imparting the knowledge of Druidism, and exhorting him to the practice of virtue.

There was still another degree to be administered to those who aspired to a high degree of perfection. To obtain this further advancement they were subjected to the most arduous purification and were committed to the tomb for nine months, where in solitude they studied theology, philosophy, cosmogony, astronomy, etc. Dr. Oliver says this was "The death and burial of the Mysteries; and on its expiration he was said to be newly born from the womb of Ceridwen, and was pronounced a regenerate person, cleansed from his former impurities by the mystical contents of her cauldron." (History of Initiation, Oliver, p. 146.)

When the period of gestation in the womb of Ceridwen was complete, as the confinement in the tomb was termed, the candidate was ready for further instruction. Another trial, however, must be braved before the highest degree of light could be conferred. The candidate, now called the "new born infant," was placed in a boat, and committed to the mercy of the waves. If he succeeded in securing a safe landing place, he was triumphantly received, and this completion of the Three Degrees made the aspirant, a "thrice born" conferring upon, him the power of inspiration and prophecy in the highest form.

The Druids maintained a high intellectual standard, for they taught their disciples astronomy, botany, anatomy, languages, medicine, etc. Thus we see the Mysteries were always repositories of Wisdom.

Freemasonry and the Druids

By W. Winwood Reade

There is a divine and hidden science whose origin can only be discovered by the wavering lights of tradition, whose doctrines and purposes are enveloped in sacred mysteries. It is now degenerated into a society of gluttons and wine-bibbers, who yawn while their Masters expound to them those emblems which have excited the wonder of the greatest philosophers of the past, and who deem that the richest gem of freemasonry, is the banquet which closes the labor of the Lodge.

And yet this order can boast of some learned and intellectual men, who endeavor to find the key to the hidden language of symbols, and who appreciate at its true value the high honors which the initiated are permitted to enjoy.

In spite of the abuses with which it has been degraded, in spite of the sneers with which the ignorant revile it, this institution still possesses much that is holy and sublime. No feelings can be compared with those which a young man feels when, attired in strange array, blind-folded, the dagger pointed to his naked left breast, he is led through the mystic labyrinth, whose intricate ways are emblematical of the toilsome wanderings of his soul.

The strains of solemn music-the mysterious words-the low knock at the portal- -the sudden blaze of light--and the strange sight which await his eyes feeble and fluttering from their long imprisonment. What awe he feels, as kneeling on his right knee, his left hand placed upon the Book of the Law, encircled by the Masters in their robes of office, and the two white wands held over his head in the form of a cross, he takes the oath of secrecy and faith, "to hail, conceal and never reveal the hidden mysteries of the fellowship" to which he is now admitted.

And what pride flushes in his heart when the secret signs and key-words are imparted to him, and when the white apron, a badge more glorious than the fabled Golden Fleece, or the Roman Eagle is tied round his waist. Surrounded by all those signs and symbols by which the ancient nations were wont to express the power and presence of God, the Mason's Lodge resembles a scene of enchantment in the midst of this wilderness which we call the world. And those who are thus assembled together in mystic robes, seem spirits of another age, who have returned to hold their hidden meetings once more in the catacombs of the Egyptian pyramids, or in the cavern-temple sacred to Mithra, or in the subterranean labyrinths of the holy Druids. The brethren seated in a circle, one of the Masters arises and advances to the midst. He relates to them a tradition of the origin of their craft.

"After the sun had descended down the seventh age from Adam before the flood of Noah, there was born unto Methusael, the son of Mehujael, a man called Lamach who took unto himself two wives. the name of the one was Adah, of the other Zillah. Now Adah his first wife, bare two sons--the one named Jabel and the other Jubal. Jabal was the inventor of geometry and the first who built houses of stone and timber, and Jubal was the inventor of music and harmony. Zillah, his second wife, bare Tubal Cain, the instructor of every artificer in brass and iron, and a daughter called Naamah who was the founder of the weaver's craft.

"All these had knowledge from above, that the Almighty would take vengeance for sin either by fire or by water, so great was the wickedness of the world. So they reasoned among themselves how they might preserve the knowledge of the sciences which they had found, and Jabal said that there were two different kinds of stone of such virtue that one would not burn and the other would not sink--the one called marble and the other latres. They then agreed to write all the science that they had found upon these stones. "After the destruction of the world, these two pillars were discovered by Hermes, the son of Shem. Then the craft of masonry began to flourish, and Nimrod was one of the earliest patrons of the art. Abraham, the son of Jerah, was skilled in the seven sciences and taught the Egyptians the science of grammar. Euclid was his pupil, and instructed them in the art of making

mighty walls and ditches to preserve their houses from the inundations of the Nile, and by geometry measured out the land, and divided it into partitions so that each man might ascertain his own property. And he it was who gave masonry the name of geometry.

"In his days, it came to pass that the sovereign and lords of the realm had gotten many sons unlawfully by other men's wives, insomuch that the land was grievously burdened with them. A council was called but no reasonable remedy was proposed. The king then ordered a proclamation to be made throughout his realms, that high rewards would be given to any man who would devise a proper method for maintaining the children. Euclid dispelled the difficulty. He thus addressed the king: 'My noble sovereign, if I may have order and government of these lord's sons, I will teach them the seven liberal sciences, whereby they may live honestly like gentlemen, provided that you will grant me power over them by virtue of your royal commission."

"This request was immediately complied with, and Euclid established a Lodge of Masons." This tale is curious as being the earliest account of an educational institution. There are various traditions of minor interest relating to the patriarchal ages and to the wanderings of the Israelites in the wilderness.

The Freemasons claim descent from that body of builders who, some from Phœnicia, and some from India, came to Jerusalem to erect the temple of Solomon. They also assert that these masons were governed by the same laws, and united by the same ties as those of the modern order, and in the initiation of a Master-mason the following tradition is related respecting the death of the Phœnician Hiram Abiff, the master architect who directed the building of the temple:

"There were fifteen fellow-craftsmen, who finding that the temple was almost finished, and that they had not received the master's word because their time was not come, agreed to extort it from their master, the skilful Hiram Abiff, on the first opportunity, that they might pass for masters in other countries and have masters' wages. Twelve recanted and the other three determined to carry out the plot. Their names were Jubela, Jubelo, and Jubelum. These three crafts knowing that it was always the master's custom at twelve at noon,

when the men were called off to refreshment, to go into the sanctum sanctorum to pray to the true and living God--they placed themselves at the three entrances to the temple, viz., at the west, south and east doors. There was no entrance in the north, because thence the sun darts no rays. Thus they waited while he made his prayer to the Lord, to have the word or grip as he came out, or his life. So Hiram came to the east door, and Jubela demanded the master's word. Hiram told him he did not receive it in such a manner but he must wait, and time and a little patience would bring him to it, for it was not in his power to deliver it except the three Grand Masters were together, viz: Solomon, King of Israel, Hiram, King of Tyre, and Hiram Abiff. "Jubela struck him across the throat with a 24-inch gauge. He fled thence to the south door where he was accosted in the same manner by Jubelo to whom he gave a similar answer, and who gave him a blow with a square upon his left breast. Hiram reeled but recovered himself, and flew to the west door where Jubelum gave him a heavy blow upon the head with a common gavel or setting maul which proved his death.

"After this they carried him out of the west door and hid him in a heap of rubbish till it was twelve at night, when they found means to bury him in a handsome grave, six feet east and west, and six feet in height. "When Hiram was missed, King Solomon made great inquiry after him, and not hearing anything of him supposed him to be dead. The twelve crafts that had recanted hearing the said report, and their consciences pricking them, went and informed King Solomon with white aprons and gloves as tokens of their innocence. King Solomon forthwith sent them in search of the three murderers who had absconded, and they agreed to make the pursuit in four parties, three going north, three south, three east, and three west.

"As one of these parties traveled down to the sea of Joppa, one of them sitting himself down to rest by the side of a rock, heard the following lamentations proceed from a cleft within:- - "'O that I had my throat cut across, and my tongue torn out by the root, and buried in the sands of the sea at low water a cable length from the shore, where the tide doth regularly ebb and flow twice in the course of the twenty- four hours, than that I had been concerned in the death of our master Hiram."

And then another voice: "'Oh! that I had my heart torn from under my naked left breast, and given to the vultures of the air as a prey, rather than I had been concerned in the death of so good a master." "'But oh!' cried Jubelum. I struck him harder than you both, for I killed him. Oh! that I had had my body severed in two, one part carried to the south, and the other to the north, my bowels burnt to ashes and scattered before the four winds of the earth, rather than I had been concerned in the death of our master Hiram." "The brother that heard these sorrowful lamentations hailed the other two, and they went into the cleft of the rock and took them and bound them, and brought them before King Solomon, when they owned what had passed, and what they had done, and did not desire to live, therefore King Solomon ordered their own sentences to be executed upon them, saying, 'They have signed their own deaths, and let it be upon them as they have said." "'Jubela was taken out, and his throat cut across, and his tongue torn out by the root, and buried in the sands of the sea at low water, a cable length from the shore, where the tide did regularly ebb and flow twice in the course of the twenty-four hours. "Jubelo's heart was torn from under his naked left breast, and was given to the vultures of the air as a prey. "Jubelum's body was severed in two, one part was carried to the north, the other to the south, his bowels were burnt to ashes and scattered to the four winds of the earth." The real secret of Freemasonry, viz., its origin and purport, as yet remain an enigma and will probably ever remain so. There are some authors who have fixed the source of this sacred and mysterious fountain within the oaken groves of the extinguished order of the Druids. Who assert that when Druidism was proscribed, its priests adopted various disguises and carried their learning into various professions. Some became school-masters and taught science to the youth of Britain, as they had once done in the forest seminaries of Mona. Some fortune-tellers, the parents of

the tribes of gypsies who still retain a kind of brotherhood united by oaths and secret signs, and who at one time possessed so strange an ascendancy over the minds of the vulgar. And others who formed themselves into a community resembling, if not in their power, at least in their unanimity, that ancient body of priests who had once been the sovereigns of Britain.

At first I was inclined to believe that such was really the case, and that Freemasonry was no more than a reproduction of Druidism in the Middle Ages. On searching for materials, I met with evidence in limine which tended to confirm me in this conviction. There was a manuscript discovered in the Bodleian Library at Oxford in 1696, which was supposed to have been written about the year 1436. It purports to be an examination of one of the brotherhood by King Henry VI, and is allowed by all masonic writers to be genuine.

Its title is as follows: "Certain questions with answers to the same concerning the mystery of masonry written by King, Henry the Sixth and faithfully copied by me John Leylande, antiquarian, by command of his highness." I give an extract modernizing the English of the original, which, though quaint, would be unintelligible to all but antiquaries:--

"What mote it be? It is the knowledge of nature, and the power of its various operations; particularly the skill of reckoning, of weights and measures, of constructing buildings and dwellings of all kinds, and the true manner of forming all things for the use of man.

"Where did it begin ?-it began with the first men of the East, who were before the first men of the West, and coming with it, it hath brought all comforts to the wild and comfortless.

"Who brought it to the West?--the Phoenicians who, being great merchants, came first from the East into Phoenicia, for the convenience of commerce, both East and West by the Red and Mediterranean Seas.

"How came it into England?--Pythagoras, a Grecian, traveled to acquire knowledge in Egypt and in Syria, and in every other land where the Phoenicians had planted masonry; and gaining admittance into all lodges of masons, he learned much, and returned and dwelt in Grecia Magna, growing and becoming mighty wise and greatly renowned. Here he formed a great lodge at Crotona, and made many masons, some of whom traveled into France, and there made many more, from whence, in process of time, the art passed into England."

This, I need not remind the reader, is a story very similar to those current respecting the first planting of Druidism in Britain. I also discovered as I thought, a key to the tradition of Hiram Abiff, which I have just related, viz., that it was simply the story of Osiris (killed by Typhon the Evil Spirit, buried in a coffin and found by Isis) so corrupted by modern Masons.

In the continuation of the story of Hiram, it is stated that the twelve crafts on discovering his body were unable to raise it, and that King Solomon ordered a lodge of master-masons to be summoned and said, "I will go myself in person and try to raise the body by the master's grip or the lion's paw." By means of this grip the Grand-Master Hiram was raised.

Now in a figure painted on a mummy at the Austin Fryar's of La Place des Victores, representing the death and resurrection of Osiris, is seen an exact model of the position of the master-mason as he raises Hiram. Jubela, Jubelo, Jubelum are merely variations from the Latin word jubeo, I command. The pretended assassins are represented as demanding the master's grip and word from Hiram in an imperious manner. A more satisfactory proof of the truth of this statement is contained in an astronomical notion of the Hindus, whose

Chrisna is the same as the Osiris of the Egyptians. The Decans, or Elohim, are the gods of whom it is said the Almighty created the Universe. They arranged the order of the zodiac. The Elohim of the summer were gods of a benevolent disposition: they made the days long, and loaded the sun's head with topaz. While the three wretches that presided in the winter at the extreme end of the year, hid in the realms below, were, with the constellation to which they belonged, cut off from the rest of the zodiac; and as they were missing, were consequently accused of bringing Chrisna into those troubles which at last ended in his death.

Even allowing these premises to be true, it does not necessarily follow that the traditional account of the building of Solomon's Temple by masons was also allegorical. And indeed there is so much that is purely Hebrew in ceremonial masonry, that one is almost forced to believe that the Freemasons of the present day are really descended from a body of architects, who, like the Dionysiacks of Asia Minor, were united into a fraternal association and who erected the temple of Solomon.

In these ceremonies, however, and in their emblems there is much also that is Druidic, and if Freemasonry did not emanate from Druidism, there can be no doubt that it sprang from the same origin. I will trace out the affinity between the Masonic Order of the Present, and the Druid Order of the Past. It shall be for the reader to decide whether these Masonic usages are vestiges of Druidism, or mere points of family resemblance.

The initiations of Masons are so similar to those of the Druids, that any Mason reading my article upon the subject must have been struck by the resemblance. The ovade wore a gold chain round his neck. And the apprentice when initiated has a silk cord, in masonic parlance a cable-tow, suspended from his throat. Like the ovade, the apprentice is blindfolded, and as the former was led through the mazes of a labyrinth, the latter is led backwards and forwards, and in various directions.

Thunder and lightning were counterfeited in the initiation of a Druid, and in that of the Royal Arch the Companions fire pistols, clash swords, overturn chairs, and roll cannon balls across the floor. The tiler stands at the door with a drawn sword.

And tests of fortitude though less severe than in former times are not unknown among Masons. The following arduous trial was used in the Female Lodges of Paris:-- "A candidate for admission was usually very much excited. During a part of the ceremony she was conducted to an eminence, and told to look down at what awaited her if she faltered in her duty. Beneath her appeared a frightful abyss in which a double row of iron spikes were visible. No doubt her mind was in a chaos of fanaticism, for instead of shrinking at the sight, she exclaimed 'I can encounter all,' and sprang forward. At that moment a secret spring was touched, and the candidate fell not on the spikes, but on a green bed in imitation of a verdant plain. She fainted but was soon recovered by her friends, when the scene having changed she was reanimated and soothed by the sweet strains of choral music."

I have already shown, I trust conclusively, that the Druidic mysteries were founded on those of the Egyptians, and were analogous to those of Tyre, Persia and Hindostan; and that their moral doctrines and pristine simplicity of worship were those of the Hebrew Patriarchs.

It will be easy to show that those of Freemasonry, if not a mere perpetuation of the Druidic were derived from the same fountains, and that the secrets of this science and philosophy are hidden from us by the veil of Isis. To the Egyptian candidate on his- initiation, the Hierophant displayed the holy volume of hieroglyphics which he then restored to its repository.

So when the eyes of the apprentice are first released from darkness, he beholds the volume of the sacred law. During the Persian initiations, the doctrine was enforced ex cathedra, from the desk or pulpit. So the Grand Master sits on a throne before which the candidate kneels, pointing a dagger to his naked left breast and two white wands being crossed above his head.

On the seal of the ancient Abbey of Arbroath in Scotland, is a representation which bears a curious resemblance to the engraving on a seal used by the priests of Isis, and which Plutarch describes in his Essay on Isis and Osiris--a man kneeling, his hands bound, and a knife at his throat.

In all the ancient mysteries before an aspirant could claim participation in the higher secrets of the institution, he was placed within the pastos or bed, or coffin, and was subjected to a confinement in darkness for a certain time. This I have described to be practiced by the Druids. In some of their labyrinths, discovered in France, the remains of cells have been found, and there was a dark cell of probation recently standing near Maidstone, Kitt's Cotti House--from Ked (or Ceridwen) the British Isis, and cotti an ark, or chest.

So in the initiation of a Master Mason, the candidate is in some lodges buried in a coffin to represent the death of the murdered Hiram Abiff. The grand festival of Masonry is on Midsummer Day, which was also the grand festival of the Druids.

The processional movements of the Masons as of the Druids were mostly circular. I have already instanced the symbol by which the Jews expressed the word 'Jehovah.' This letter jod was believed by them to denote the presence of God, especially when conveyed in a circle.

Masons also have a word which they are not allowed to pronounce except in the presence of a full lodge, and they pay peculiar reverence to a point within a circle. Some of the Druidic monuments are simple circles with a stone standing in the midst, and the boss in the centre of their circular shields had probably the same signification.

The Masonic Lodge, like all Pagan temples, is built due east and west. Its form is an oblong square which the ancients believed to be the shape of the world. In the west are two pillars surmounted by globes. The one on the left is called Boaz, and is supposed to represent Osiris or the sun, the other Jachin, the emblem of Isis or the moon. The floor is mosaic, and the walls are adorned with the various symbols of the craft.

The cross is one of the chief emblems in Masonry as it was in Druidism, and in all the Pagan religions. The Taw is a badge in Royal Arch Masonry, and almost all the other varieties of the symbol are used in Masonry. The key and the cross-keys are also mosaic symbols. They are supposed to be astronomical signs of Anubis, or the Dog-Star.

An ear-of-corn is a prominent emblem in Masonry, proving that the order did not confine their intellects and their labors to the building of houses, but devoted themselves also to agriculture. A sprig of acacia is one of the emblems revered by the Masons, and answers to the Egyptian lotus, to the myrtle of Eleusis, to the golden branch of Virgil and to the Druidic mistletoe. It is curious that Houzza which Mahomet esteemed an idol--Houzza so honored in the Arabian works of Ghatfân

Koreisch, Kenanah and Salem should be simply the acacia. Thence was derived the word huzza! in our language, which was probably at first a religious exclamation like the Evohe! of the Bacchantes. The doctrines of Masonry are the most beautiful that it is possible to conceive. They breathe the simplicity of the earliest ages animated by the love of a martyred God.

That word which the Puritans translated "charity," but which is really "love"-- love is the key-stone of the Royal Arch upon which is supported the entire system of this mystic science. In the lectures of the French Lodges the whole duty of a Mason is summed up in this one brief sentence: "Aimez-vous les uns les autres, instruisez-vous, secourez-vous, voilà tout noire livre, toute noire loi, toule noire science."

"Love one another, teach one another, help one another. That is all our doctrine, all our science, all our law." Ah! rail against us bigoted and ignorant men, slander us curious and jealous women if you will. Those who obey the precepts of their masters, and those who listen to the truths which they inculcate can readily forgive you. It is impossible to be a good Mason without being a good man.

We have no narrow-minded prejudices; we do not debar from our society this sect, or that sect; it is sufficient for us that a man worships God, no matter under what name or in what manner, and we admit him. Christians, Jews, Muslims, Buddhists are enrolled among us, and it is in the Mason's Lodge alone that they can kneel down together without feeling hatred, without professing contempt against their brother worshippers.

www.ingramcontent.com/pod-product-compliance
Lightning Source LLC
LaVergne TN
LVHW041458070426
835507LV00009B/677